Josef SUK

FANTASTICKÉ SCHERZO
Op. 25
(1903)

SERENISSIMA MUSIC, INC.

INSTRUMENTATION

2 Flutes

Piccolo

2 Oboes

English Horn

2 Clarinets in B-flat and A

Bass Clarinet in B-flat

2 Bassoons

4 Horns in F

2 Trumpets in C

3 Trombones

Tuba

Timpani

Percussion
(Triangle, Tambourine, Cymbals)

Harp

Violin I

Violin II

Viola

Violoncello

Bass

Duration: ca. 15 minutes

ISBN: 1-932419-07-1
ISMN M-800001-07-9

This score is a slightly modified unabridged reprint of the
score published ca. 1905 by Breitkopf & Härtel, Leipzig.
The score has been reduced to fit the present format.

Printed in the USA
First Printing: July, 2004

FANTASTICKÉ SCHERZO
SCHERZO FANTASTIQUE

JOSEF SUK, Op. 25
(1874–1935)

SERENISSIMA MUSIC, INC.

7

16

20

24

28

* *fp* e *fz* ben accentare

* Tutti trilli senza cadenza

34

36

42

*sempre con accento acuto

45

46

50

52

53

57

60

64

74

77

80